Loving a Woman
in Two Worlds

Books by Robert Bly

Poems
Silence in the Snowy Fields
The Light Around the Body
Sleepers Joining Hands
The Morning Glory
This Tree Will Be Here for a Thousand Years
This Body Is Made of Camphor and Gopher Wood
The Man in the Black Coat Turns
Translations
Selected Poems of Rainer Maria Rilke
Times Alone: Selected Poems of Antonio Machado
Neruda and Vallejo: Selected Poems
Lorca and Jiménez: Selected Poems
The Kabir Book
Criticism and Anthologies
Talking All Morning
Leaping Poetry
News of the Universe

Loving a Woman in Two Worlds

ROBERT BLY

The Dial Press
Doubleday & Company, Inc.,
Garden City, New York
1985

Library of Congress Cataloging in Publication Data

Bly, Robert.
  Loving a woman in two worlds.

  1. Love poetry, American.   I. Title.
PS3552.L9L6 1985   811'.54   84-12704
ISBN 0-385-27418-1

Published by The Dial Press
Copyright © 1985 by Robert Bly
All Rights Reserved
Manufactured in the United States of America
First Printing

Acknowledgments

I am grateful to the editors of the following reviews, in whose pages some of these poems first appeared: *Plainsong, The Georgia Review, Ploughshares, Harvard Magazine, American Poetry Review, Ohio Review, Poetry East, New Age, The New Republic, The Atlantic Monthly, ReVision, Ironwood, The Kenyon Review, Poetry, Forum, Aloe, The Cow Creek Review, Silent Voices,* and *The Walt Whitman Review.* The poems "On Sleep" and "The Indigo Bunting" were first published in *The New Yorker.* Red Ozier Press, Calliope Press, and Ally Press each published some of these poems in booklet form, and I am grateful to the respective editors as well for permission to reprint here.

Contents

Loving a Woman
in Two Worlds

ONE

Fifty Males Sitting Together

After a long walk in the woods clear cut for lumber,
lit up by a few young pines,
I turn home,
drawn to water. A coffinlike band
softens half the lake,
draws the shadow
down from westward hills.
It is a massive
masculine shadow,
fifty males sitting together
in hall or crowded room,
lifting something indistinct
up into the resonating night.

Sunlight kindles the water still free of shadow,
kindles it till it glows with the high
pink of wounds.

Reeds stand about in groups
unevenly as if they might
finally ascend
to the sky all together!
Reeds protect
the band near shore.
Each reed has its own thin
thread of darkness inside;
it is relaxed and rooted in the black
mud and snail shells under the sand.

The woman stays in the kitchen, and does not want
to waste fuel by lighting a lamp,
as she waits
for the drunk husband to come home.
Then she serves him
food in silence.
What does the son do?
He turns away,
loses courage,
goes outdoors to feed with wild
things, lives among dens
and huts, eats distance and silence,
he grows long wings, enters the spiral, ascends.

How far he is from working men when he ascends!
From all men! The males singing
chant far out
on the water grounded in downward shadow.
He cannot go there because

4

he has not grieved
as humans grieve. If someone
died, whose
head was cut off?
The father's? Or the mother's? Or his?
The dark comes down slowly, the way
snow falls, or herds pass a cave mouth.
I look up at the other shore; it is night.

The Indigo Bunting

I go to the door often.
Night and summer. Crickets
lift their cries.
I know you are out.
You are driving
late through the summer night.

I do not know what will happen.
I have no claim on you.
I am one star
you have as guide; others
love you, the night
so dark over the Azores.

You have been working outdoors,
gone all week. I feel you

in this lamp lit
so late. As I reach for it
I feel myself
driving through the night.

I love a firmness in you
that disdains the trivial
and regains the difficult.
You become part then
of the firmness of night,
the granite holding up walls.

There were women in Egypt who
supported with their firmness the stars
as they revolved,
hardly aware
of the passage from night
to day and back to night.

I love you where you go
through the night, not swerving,
clear as the indigo
bunting in her flight,
passing over two
thousand miles of ocean.

"Out of the Rolling Ocean, the Crowd . . ."

It is not only the ant that walks on the carpenter's
       board alone,
nor the March turtle on his boulder surrounded by
       March water . . .
I know there are whitecaps that are born and
       die alone,
and a rocky pasture, and a new one nearby, with a
       path between.
There are branchy stalks, dropped to the ground
       last summer,
and tires, half worn-down, lifted to the gas-station-
       owner's rack.
All of them I saw today, and all of them were dear
       to me,
and the rough-barked young cottonwood alone on the
       windy shore.

Behind matter there is some kind of heat, around and
           behind things,
so that what we experience is not the turtle nor
           the night
only, nor the rising whirlwind, nor the certainty, nor
           the steady gaze,
nor the meeting by the altar, nor the rising sun only.

The Whole Moisty Night

The Viking ship sails into the full harbor.
The body meets its wife far out at sea.
Its lamp remains lit the whole moisty night.
Water pours down, faint flute notes in the sound of
       the water.

Secrets

I walk below the over-bending birches,
birches that arch together in the air.
It is an omen of an open door,
a fear no longer found in the wind.
Are there unions only the earth sees?
The birches live where no one else comes,
deep in the unworried woods . . .
These sandgrains looked at by deer bellies.

Letter to Her

What I did I did.
I knew that I loved you
and told you that.
Then I lied to you
often so you would love me,
hid the truth,
shammed, lied.

Once human beings
in their way do what they do
they find peakéd
castles ahead, they see
lanterns aloft over
the seal-like masses
where they love at night.

The hurricane carries
off the snail, still
clinging to his pine
tree. At night the o-
possum sees the golden
lion upside
down in his dream.

To do what we do
does not mean joy. The sun
rises, and some-
thing strong guides the sun
over the sky until
it carries its spark down
to the northern forests.

Two People at Dawn

The sun orange and rose
lights up covers and clouds.
Her head lies in his lap.
And his hand curves around
the bone box of her head.
Odor of candles
floats in the room.

He says, "Our river flows
on a black mud bottom.
Are we walking there?
Are we under water?"
"We are under the ocean."
"Ah well," he says, "the ocean
is only a slow river."

His hand remains firm.
Her courage shines
the whole length of her body.
The man joins her
in that briny place
where cattle graze
on grass below the water.

Winter Poem

The quivering wings of the winter ant
wait for lean winter to end.
I love you in slow, dim-witted ways,
hardly speaking, one or two words only.

What caused us each to live hidden?
A wound, the wind, a word, a parent.
Sometimes we wait in a helpless way,
awkwardly, not whole and not healed.

When we hid the wound, we fell back
from a human to a shelled life.
Now we feel the ant's hard chest,
the carapace, the silent tongue.

This must be the way of the ant,
the winter ant, the way of those
who are wounded and want to live:
to breathe, to sense another, and to wait.

In Rainy September

In rainy September, when leaves grow down to the
      dark,
I put my forehead down to the damp, seaweed-
      smelling sand.
The time has come. I have put off choosing for years,
perhaps whole lives. The fern has no choice but to
      live;
for its stubbornness it receives earth, water, and
      night.

We close the door. "I have no claim on you."
Dusk comes. "The love I have had with you is
      enough."
We know we could live apart from one another.
The sheldrake floats apart from the flock.
The oaktree puts out leaves alone on the lonely
      hillside.

Men and women before us have accomplished this.
I would see you, and you me, once a year.
We would be two kernels, and not be planted.
We stay in the room, door closed, lights out.
I weep with you without shame and without honor.

A Third Body

A man and a woman sit near each other, and they do
      not long
at this moment to be older, or younger, nor born
in any other nation, or time, or place.
They are content to be where they are, talking or
      not-talking.
Their breaths together feed someone whom we do
      not know.
The man sees the way his fingers move;
he sees her hands close around a book she hands
      to him.
They obey a third body that they share in common.
They have made a promise to love that body.
Age may come, parting may come, death will come.
A man and a woman sit near each other;
as they breathe they feed someone we do not know,
someone we know of, whom we have never seen.

No Mountain Peak Without Its Rolling Foothills

A man and a woman linger under a tree,
soberly, standing near his horse.
The low muttering speech instinct makes
to instinct remains hearable and unhearable.
The canoe shoots down the narrow channel,
the climber goes rock to rock up the mountainside.
The horses, hair blowing, disappear into the storm.

Finding Sharks' Teeth in a Rock

The cabin of the early snail swerves and falls
through miles of murky stuff, and the shark, turning,
swerves, one fin working, finally settles,
joins the rock, serves. When I strike it hard,
teeth delicate as black kites fall out!
So it is, has been. Sharks' teeth glitter
in the light of the old moon. It was to her
the Chaldean horns shot out their cry at dawn,
mingling our uneasy cries with the containing rocks.

TWO

The Roots

Finally in the bear's cabin I come to earth.
There are limits. Among all the limits
we *know* so few things. How is it that I know
only one river—its turns—and one woman?
The love of woman is the knowing of grief.
There are no limits to grief. The loving man
simmers his porcupine stew. Among the tim-
ber growing on earth grief finds roots.

What Frightened Us

Drops of rain fall into black fields.
Leaves fallen on the highway remain
where they fall, and resist the wind.
A power neither of us knows has spoken to us.

All night rain came in. We had descended
yesterday to some inner, or innermost cave,
and this—as we woke today with faces wet
from overnight rain—frightens us a little.

Smoke of rain lifts from gravel roads.
Rain water gathers below the barns.
Other waters slowly join in woods.
Silent in the moonlight, no beginning or end.

Seeing You Carry Plants In

How much I love you. The night is moist.
The air is still, as when I love you.
It is not every evening that I love you.
I come back like the stars, sometimes out of clouds.

The night is moist, and nourishing as your mind
that lets everything around you live.
I saw you carry the plants inside tonight
over the grass, to save them from the cold.

Sometimes I slip behind a door, so that
I will not be called on, or walk
hunched on sandbars below earth, not sure
if anyone in my family can love.

Your voice is water open beneath stars,
collected from abundant rain, gone to low places.
The night is moist, the ground wet,
air still, trees silent, and tonight I love you.

The Two Rivers

Inside us there is a river born in the good cold
that longs to give itself to the Gulf of light.
And there is another river more like the Missouri
that carries earth, and earth joys, and the earthly.

Come with Me

We walk together in willows, among willows.
The cowrie shell has its rosy mouth;
the tree nods and rises;
the conch returns to the dark waters.

Come with me, we will walk alone,
away from the buildings and the high places.
I love to go with you,
and enter the valley where no one is king.

At Midocean

All day I loved you in a fever, holding on to the tail
    of the horse.
I overflowed whenever I reached out to touch you.
My hand moved over your body, covered
with its dress,
burning, rough, an animal's foot or hand moving
    over leaves.
The rainstorm retires, clouds open, sunlight
sliding over ocean water a thousand miles from land.

In the Time of Peony Blossoming

When I come near the red peony flower
I tremble as water does near thunder,
as the well does when the plates of earth move,
or the tree when fifty birds leave at once.

The peony says that we have been given a gift,
and it is not the gift of this world.
Behind the leaves of the peony
there is a world still darker, that feeds many.

Night Frogs

I wake and find myself in the woods, far from
        the castle.
The train hurtles through lonely Louisiana at night.
The sleeper turns to the wall, delicate
aircraft dive toward earth.

A woman whispers to me, urges me to speak truths.
"I am afraid that you won't be honest with me."
Half or more of the moon rolls on in shadow.
Owls talk at night, loons wheel cries through
        lower waters.

Hoof marks turn up—something with hooves
        tramples
the grasses while the horses are asleep.
A shape flat and four feet long slips under the door
and lies exhausted on the floor in the morning.

When I look back, there is a blind spot in the car.
What is it in my father I keep not noticing?
I cannot remember years of my childhood.
Some parts of me I cannot find now.

I intended that; I threw some parts of me away
at ten; others at twenty; a lot at twenty-eight.
I wanted to thin myself out as a wire is thinned.
Is there enough left of me now to be honest?

The lizard moves stiffly over November roads.
How much I am drawn toward my parents!
       I walk back
and forth, looking toward the old landing.
Night frogs give out the croak of the planet turning.

The March Buds

They lie on the bed, hearing music.
The perfumed pillow, the lake, a woman's laughter.
Wind blows faintly, touches the March buds.
The young trees sway back and forth.

The Turtle

Rain lifts the lake level, washing the reeds.
Slowly the milkweed pods open, the yellow lily pads.
Through the mist man and woman see the far shore.
The turtle's head rises out over the water.

Such Different Wants

The board floats on the river.
The board wants nothing
but is pulled from beneath
on into deeper waters.

And the elephant dwelling
on the mountain wants
a trumpet so its dying cry
can be heard by the stars.

The wakeful heron striding
through reeds at dawn wants
the god of sun and moon
to see his long skinny neck.

You must say what you want.
I want to be the man
and I am who will love you
when your hair is white.

Ferns

It was among ferns I learned about eternity.
Below your belly there is a curly place.
Through you I learned to love the ferns on that bank,
and the curve the deer's hoof leaves in sand.

The Hummingbird Valley

I love to come near the hummingbird valley,
that place where we have played so often.
It is a garden where the night-hummingbirds live,
hovering in the night on fast wings.

Hills on each side close in that garden,
immaculate as the mouse's fur;
there the hummingbirds come to the plum trees,
and the plums lie about on the darkening earth.

Isn't it a house? It has been a house to me.
The cantor waits to enter the synagogue—
more than a garden—and I hear the slow oceany
chanting of the Babylonian masses.

And with what interest I hear the hummingbird
        listening
to words about to be spoken for the first time.
They bless all hummingbirds, and they bless this
        house
where we first exchanged salt and bread together.

Love Poem in Twos and Threes

What kind of people
are these? Some stammer
of land, some
want nothing but light—
no house or land
thrown away for a woman,
no ample recklessness.
How much I need
a woman's soul, felt
in my own knees,
shoulders and hands.
I was born sad!
I am a northern goat
of winter light,
up to my knees in snow.
Standing by you, I am
glad as the clams
at high tide, eerily
content as the amorous
ocean owls.

Returning Poem

Men bring the boat at night inside its slanted house
      by the shore;
goats return when the farmer calls them to their
      earth-barn at night.
Brothers, working on different farms, go home
      after dark
and sleep together at last in the attic room under its
      slanting roof.
And the deer returns, finding her way through woods
      to her curving grass.

At night the man goes to the bus to meet the woman
      he loves—
it has only been a day—and impatiently brings
      her home.

So what was far out into the air, and the longitudes of
      the earth
is brought home, taken in, a place prepared in
      the chest,
and the mountain loon returns, and soon is asleep in
      the mountain lake.

The Minty Grass

The ram walks over the minty grass.
The hawk ruffles his shoulder feathers.
Two chooks sit with feathers overlapping.
Just before dark big snowflakes fall.

Night Winds

Night winds sway the lilacs near the abandoned
      woodshed.
I am alone now; trees dark; the time for heroes is
      over.
Night winds pull me out; I am pulled away from day;
I float in the current, calm and mad as a sleepy cork.

All afternoon, lying on a hill of kisses and fever,
we felt winds around us, below us, above us,
holding us where we want to be, and I live now
surrounded by those swirls as an island by
      smoky water.

I sway like the branches, and do not choose
      the motion.
I am faithful as the ant with his small waist.
What do heroes and Hercules mean to me now?
I will remain here; you will find me where you
      left me.

Alone a Few Hours

Today I was alone a few hours, and slowly
windows darkened, leaving me alone, naked,
with no father or uncle,
born in no country . . . I was a streak of light
through the sky,
a trail in the snow behind the field mouse,
a thing that has
simple desires, and one
or two needs, like a barn darkened by rain.

Something enters from the open window.
I sense it, and turn slightly
to the left. Then I notice
shadows are dear to me, shadows in the weeds
near the lake,
and under the writing table where I sit
writing this.
"The hermit is not here;
he is up on the mountain picking ferns."

That's what the hermit's boy told the visitor
looking for him. Then I realize that I do love,
at last, that the simple
joy of the field mouse has come to me.
I am no longer
a stone pile visited from below
by the old ones.
"It's misty up there . . .
I don't know where he is . . . I don't think you can
        find him."

The Moose

The Arctic moose drinks at the tundra's edge,
swirling the watercress with his mouth.
How fresh the water is, the coolness of the far North.
A light wind moves through the deep firs.

Mountain Grass

Rain falls on mountain grass; we remain close all day.
The fuchsia lifts its tendrils high.
I need you, to hold you, as mountain grass holds rain.
Dampness falls on dampness; rain on wet earth.
I am the traveller on the mountain who keeps
       repeating his cry.

What We Provide

Every breath taken in by the man
who loves, and the woman who loves,
goes to fill the water tank
where the spirit horses drink.

Poem on Sleep

"Then the bright being disguised as a seal dove into
   the deep billows."
I go on loving you after we are asleep.
I know the ledges where we sit all night looking out
   over the briny sea,
and the open places where we coast in sleekness
   through the sea.

And where is the hunter who is cunning? The
   practical part of me?
Oh he is long since gone, dispersed among the
   bold grasses.
The one he does not know of remains afloat and
   awake all night;
he lies on luminous boulders, dives, his coat sleek, his
   eyes open.

The Artist at Fifty

The crow nests high in the fir.
Birds leap through the snowy branches
uttering small cries. Clumps fall.
Mice run dragging their tails in the new-fallen snow.

Year after year the artist works,
early and late, studying the old.
What does he gain? Finally he dreams
one night of deer antlers abandoned in the snow.

Words Barely Heard

The bear in his heavy fur rises from the bed.
The extravagant one he has left behind murmurs . . .
Or is murmured . . . Words barely heard.
Her face shines; and he turns back toward her.

The Conditions

What we have loved is with us ever,
ever, ever!
So you are with me far into the past,
the oats of Egypt . . .
I was a black hen!
You were the grain of wheat
I insisted on
before I agreed to be born.

A Man and a Woman and a Blackbird

A man and a woman
are one.
A man and a woman and a blackbird
are one.

Wallace Stevens

When the two rivers
join in the cloudy chamber,
so many alien nights
in our twenties, alone
on interior mountains,
forgotten. Blackbirds
walk around our feet
as if they shared
in what we know.

We know and we don't know
what the heron feels
with his wing-
tip feathers stretched
out in the air above
the flooded lake,
or the odorous constellations
the pig sees
past his wild snout.
A man and a woman
sit near each other. On
the windowpane
ice.
The man says: "How
is it
I have never loved
ice before?
If I have not loved ice,
what have I loved?
Loved the dead
in their Sumerian
fish-cloaks?
The vultures celebrating?
The soldiers
and the poor?"
And yet
for one or two
moments,
in our shared grief
and exile,

we hang our harps
on the willows,
and the willows
join us,
and the man
and the woman
and the blackbird are one.

THREE

The Minnow Turning

Once I loved you only a few minutes a day.
Now it is smoke rising, the mushroom left by
            the birch,
and horse's forefoot, the way the minnow stirs silver
as he turns, carrying his world with him.

Firmness

My fierceness when I hold you belongs
to the fir logs rolling on the shore.
And your affections coming toward me are the
          Oregon
islands disappearing in surf and mist.

Conversation

I sat beneath maples, reading,
a book in my lap, alone all morning.
You walked past—whom I have loved
for ten years—walked by and were gone.

That was all. When I returned
to reading, not all of me returned.
My sex, or rosy man,
reached on its own and touched the book.

It must be some words have fur.
Or mute things exchange thought.
Or perhaps I am no longer
weary, grieving, and alone.

We know it's true: the bee's foot
knows the anther and its dwarves,
as the castle of women knows
of the rider lost outside in the trees.

Shame

A man and a woman sit
among firs, looking eastward.
Sun is rising. Wind
from behind them lifts
them and carries them
over the fir needles.
They whirl, and the motion
carries them
down through the narrow
opening at the center.
Through it each must
pass, with toes curled out,
arms thrown back,
all shame gone.

The Horse of Desire

"Yesterday I saw a face
that gave off light."
I wrote that the first time
I saw you; now the lines
written that morning
are twenty years old.
What is it that
we see and don't see?

When a horse swings
his head, how easily
his shoulders follow.
When the right thing happens,
the whole body knows.
The road covered with stones
turns to a soft river
moving among reeds.

I love you in those reeds,
and in the bass
quickening there.
My love is in the demons
gobbling the waters,
my desire in their swollen
foreheads poking
earthward out of the trees.

The bear between my legs
has one eye only,
which he offers
to God to see with.
The two beings below with no
eyes at all love you
with the slow persistent
intensity of the blind.

Listening to the Köln Concert

After we had loved each other intently,
we heard notes tumbling together,
in late winter, and we heard ice
falling from the ends of twigs.

The notes abandon so much as they move.
They are the food not eaten, the comfort
not taken, the lies not spoken.
The music is my attention to you.

And when the music came again,
later in the day, I saw tears in your eyes.
I saw you turn your face away
so that the others would not see.

When men and women come together,
how much they have to abandon! Wrens
make their nests of fancy threads
and string ends, animals

abandon all their money each year.
What is that men and women leave?
Harder than wrens' doing, they have
to abandon their longing for the perfect.

The inner nest not made by instinct
will never be quite round,
and each has to enter the nest
made by the other imperfect bird.

Conversation with a Holy Woman
Not Seen for Many Years

After so many years, I come walking to you.
You say: "You have come after so long?"
I could not come earlier. My shabby mouth,
with its cavernous thirst, ate the seeds of longing
that should have been planted. Awkward and baffled,
dishonest, I slept. And I dreamt of sand.
Your eyes in sorrow do not laugh.
I say, "I have come after so many years."

What Moves and Doesn't Move

At night desire and longing enter, and we feel water
hurrying through a grassy place.
By dawn we know
all minglings, things of sorrow,
rings of Saturn, the raccoon's wrist-joints and his
        smooth tail.

This is not Mozart, but a music more vulgar
        and grand.
Laughing we see the lizard hurry
to become a mammal,
or go back to the worm, or be a bird.
It is early spring; fronds rise; the frog leaps here
        and there.

Outdoors the dawn drifts restless with all its odors,
from tree to tree, between the insects,
among the stars,
leaping from twig to twig.
I am with you, held always moving in the night
    valley.

Water

The bird dips to take some water in its bill.
You know we do not drink only with our hands.
We receive what nothing else can give.
We are thirsty for the heron
and the lake, the touch of the bill on the water.

The Good Silence

Reading an Anglo-Saxon love poem in its
      extravagance,
I stand up and walk about the room.
I do not love you in a little way;
oh yes, I do love you in a little way,
the old way, the way of the rowboat alone in
      the ocean.

The image is a white-washed house, on David's Head,
      in Wales,
surrounded by flowers, bordered by seashells
and withies. A horse appears at the door
minutes before a storm; the house stands
in a space awakened by salt wind, alone on its cliff.

I take your hand as we work, neither of us speaking.
This is the old union of man and woman,
nothing extraordinary; they both feel a deep
calm in the bones. It is ordinary affection
that our bodies experienced for ten thousand years.

During those years we stroked the hair of the old,
                    brought in
roots, painted prayers, slept, laid hair
on fire, took lives, and the bones
of the dead gleamed from under rocks where the love
the roaming tribe gave them made them shine
                    at night.

And we did what we did, made love attentively, then
dove into the river, and our bodies joined as calmly
as the swimmer's shoulders glisten at dawn,
as the pine tree stands in the rain at the edge of
                    the village.
The affection rose on a slope century after century,

And one day my faithfulness to you was born.
We sit together silently at the break of day.
We sit an hour, then tears run down my face.
"What is the matter?" you say, looking over.
I answer, "The ship saileth on the salte foam."

The Hawk

The hawk sweeps down from his aerie,
dives among swallows,
turns over twice in the air,
flying out of Catal-Huyuk.
Slowly a seeing hawk
frees itself from the fog;
its sleek head sees far off.

And the ocean turns in,
gives birth to herring
oriented to the poles.
Oregon fir needles, pungent
as the proverbs of old men,
ride down the Rogue River,
enter the ocean currents.

Land and sea mingle, so we
mingle with sky and wind. A mole
told me that his mother
had gone into the sky,
and his father lay curled
in a horsechestnut shell.
And my brother is part of the ocean.

Our great-uncles, grandfathers,
great-grandfathers, remain.
While we lie asleep, they see
the grasshopper resting
on the grass blade, and the wolverine
sweeping with his elegant
teeth through the forest.

And they come near. Whenever
we talk with a small
child, the dead help us
to choose words. Choosing words,
courage comes. When a man
encouraged by the dead goes
where he wishes to go,

then he sees the long tongue
of water on which the whale
rides on his journey.
When he finds the way
long intended for him,
he tastes through glacial water
the Labrador ferns and snows.

In the Month of May

In the month of May when all leaves open,
I see when I walk how well all things
lean on each other, how the bees work,
the fish make their living the first day.
Monarchs fly high; then I understand
I love you with what in me is unfinished.

I love you with what in me is still
changing, what has no head or arms
or legs, what has not found its body.
And why shouldn't the miraculous,
caught on this earth, visit
the old man alone in his hut?

And why shouldn't Gabriel, who loves honey,
be fed with our own radishes and walnuts?
And lovers, tough ones, how many there are
whose holy bodies are not yet born.
Along the roads, I see so many places
I would like us to spend the night.